W9-CMF-066

DISCARD

THE PONY EXPRESS

JOSEPH J. DICERTO

THE PONY EXPRESS

HOOFBEATS IN THE WILDERNESS

Franklin Watts
New York/London/Toronto/Sydney
A First Book/1989

Photographs courtesy of:
The Granger Collection: cover, pp. 8, 12 (top), 22, 29, 44, 52, 55;
Wyoming State Archives, Museums and Historical Department: pp. 12
(bottom), 18 (top), 27; Pony Express Museum, St. Joseph, Mo.:
16–17, 18 (bottom), 21, 24, 25 (bottom), 32, 39 (top), 42, 48;
New York Public Library Picture Collection: p. 25 (top); Utah
State Historical Society: p. 39 (bottom); The Bettmann Archive:
p. 56; Kansas State Historical Society: p. 59.

Library of Congress Cataloging in Publication Data

DiCerto, Joseph J.
The Pony Express : hoofbeats in the wilderness / by Joseph J.
DiCerto.
    p.   cm.—(A First book)
Bibliography: p.
Includes index.
Summary: Describes the circumstances under which the Pony Express was
founded, how it was organized, the rough territory and general hardships
faced by the riders, and the technological innovation that ended it.
ISBN 0-531-10751-5
1. Pony express—History—Juvenile literature. 2. Postal service—United
States—History—Juvenile literature. [1. Pony express.] I. Title. II. Series.
HE6375.P65D53 1989
383'.143'0973—dc19   88-34548   CIP AC

CONTENTS

Chapter One
The Right Time in History
9

Chapter Two
A Dream Becomes a Reality
11

Chapter Three
Putting It All Together
14

Chapter Four
The Challenge of the Land
20

Chapter Five
The Journey and the Adventure
31

Chapter Six
Heroes on Horses
41

Chapter Seven
Passing into History
54

For Further Reading 61

Index 62

*To my wonderful son,
David Joseph,
whose sights are set
on the frontiers
of creativity.*

———————

*A special thank you to
Mrs. Jacqueline Lewin
of the Pony Express
Museum, for her
valuable help in
gathering information
for this book.*

*New Orleans was a prime example of
a bustling, nineteenth-century city
where transportation and industry
were rapidly developing.*

1 THE RIGHT TIME IN HISTORY

The Pony Express was one of the most exciting and adventurous episodes of early American history. To this day, the stories of the brave riders who carried the U.S. mail across the life-threatening wilderness remind us that the settlement of the West was made possible by people of great character and foresight, who were ready to make the supreme sacrifice for their country. The demand for the Pony Express was created because of the fast-moving developments that were occurring during that period of American history.

The United States in the early 1800s was a kaleidoscope of rapidly developing activities. People were moving west. Cities were getting bigger. Industries were expanding. Transportation and communications were developing at high speed, and extreme political views were beginning to evolve in different parts of our young nation.

The lands east of the Missouri were well settled. But for many people, there was too much civilization, too much crowding, not enough opportunity to acquire one's own land, and so, they migrated to the West.

In the year of the Pony Express (1860), the United States was in a great crisis. News-making events, regarding the civil war to come, occurred rapidly, and needed to be immediately reported to the population of California and Oregon. An express mail service was needed desperately.

2 A DREAM BECOMES A REALITY

A flow of up-to-date news and information needed to be maintained between the East and the West. There was no problem of communications between the northern industrial states and the Midwest. Stagecoach lines, steam-engine trains, and even a telegraph line brought a daily flood of news as far west as St. Joseph, Missouri. But after that, the flow became an infrequent trickle.

The explosive situation existing between the North and the South demanded drastic solutions that included a heroic attempt to establish a fast central-route mail service. And that necessity gave birth to the idea of the Pony Express.

In the winter of 1860, Mr. William Russell, the senior partner of Russell, Majors and Waddell, was

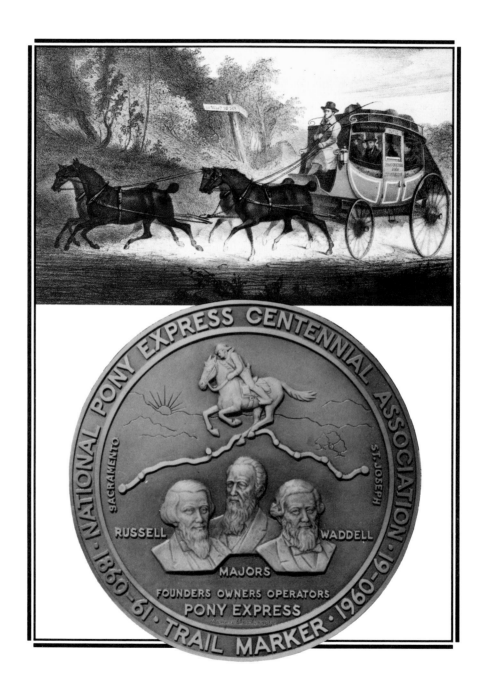

called to Washington on business where he met with Senator Gwin of California, who enthusiastically described the idea of a central-route mail service. Russell, immediately recognizing the value of such a service, and believing that it would lead to a very lucrative government contract, committed his company to establishing the Pony Express. But it was now January, and the mail service was to be started in April, a very short time in which to do a great deal of work. Russell raced back to Fort Leavenworth, Kansas, to confer with his partners. To his surprise, Alexander Majors and William Waddell did not like the idea at all, pointing out that such an undertaking would be extremely expensive and unprofitable at best.

However, since Russell had already committed the company to the project, the argument was settled. The Pony Express was to be started.

Above: Before the Pony Express, stagecoach lines carried the news from city to city. Below: A plaque commemorating the Pony Express's centennial.

3 PUTTING IT ALL TOGETHER

Finding themselves committed to the job of building an almost 2,000 mile (3,218 km) express mail route, and with a mere three months in which to accomplish the task, the trio of Russell, Majors, and Waddell plunged into the project. They set up a separate corporation first, purchased a number of mail routes, and bought a large passenger and freighting business. The plan was to establish a route that basically followed the old Oregon Trail. The service would start at St. Joseph, Missouri and pass through Kansas, Nebraska, Colorado, Wyoming, Utah, and Nevada, and end in San Francisco, California, a distance of 1,840 miles (2,960 km).

The service guaranteed the delivery of mail (no packages were carried) from St. Joseph, Missouri to San Francisco in an incredible ten days. In order to accomplish this, the riders would have to drive their horses at top speed, with a change of animals occurring every 10 to 20 (16–32 km) miles. These locations were called relay stations. They were mostly rough, simple cabins, with a few stalls and a corral to maintain the change horses. They were staffed by a stationkeeper and one or two helpers who took care of the livestock and did the necessary daily chores. Pony Express riders rarely spent more than two minutes at these stations, just enough time to leap off their horses, throw the *mochila* (leather saddle bag that held the mail) over the saddle of a fresh mount, leap into the saddle, and wave good-bye as they sped off on their appointed run. The stationkeeper had complete responsibility for the facility. Not only did he have to supervise the care of the livestock and the maintenance of the station, he also had to order supplies, be certain that a change horse was saddled and ready for the incoming rider, and keep an accurate record of the rider's arrival and departure times. Working at one of the remote stations often located in hostile territory was a lonesome and dangerous occupa-

OREGON

IDAHO TERRITORY
(Statehood in 1890)

Snake River

NEVADA

CALIFORNIA

UTAH TERRITORY

Colorado River

ARIZONA TERRITORY
(Statehood in 1912)

Sacramento

Mills
Folsom
Mass
Placerville
Sportsman's Hall
Strawberry
Webster's
Yanks
Friday's
Carson
Genoa
Dayton
Nevada
Old River
Reed's Station
Stillwater
Busby's
Fairview
Sand Springs
Gold Springs
Middle Creek
Castle Rock
Edward's Creek
Jacobville
Mt. Airy
Simpson's Park
Cape Horn
Dry Creek
Sulfur Springs
Camp Station
Jacob's Well
Roberts Creek
Mountain Springs
Diamond Springs
Shell Creek
Egan Butte
Ruby Valley
Spring Valley
Prairie Gate
Antelope Springs
Canyon
Willow Springs
Boyd's
Fish Spring
Black Rock
Simpson's Springs
River Bed
Dug Way
Point Lookout
Faust's
Rush Valley
Pass
Crittenden
Joe Dugout
Rockwell's
Traveler's Rest
Snyder's
Salt Lake City
Mtn Dell
Dixie
Weber
Echo
Heneler
Hanging Rock
Needle Rock
Quaking Asp
Bear River
Maddy
Millersville
Church Buttes
Ham's Fork
Green River
Big Bend
Big Sandy
Ft. Bridger
Granger

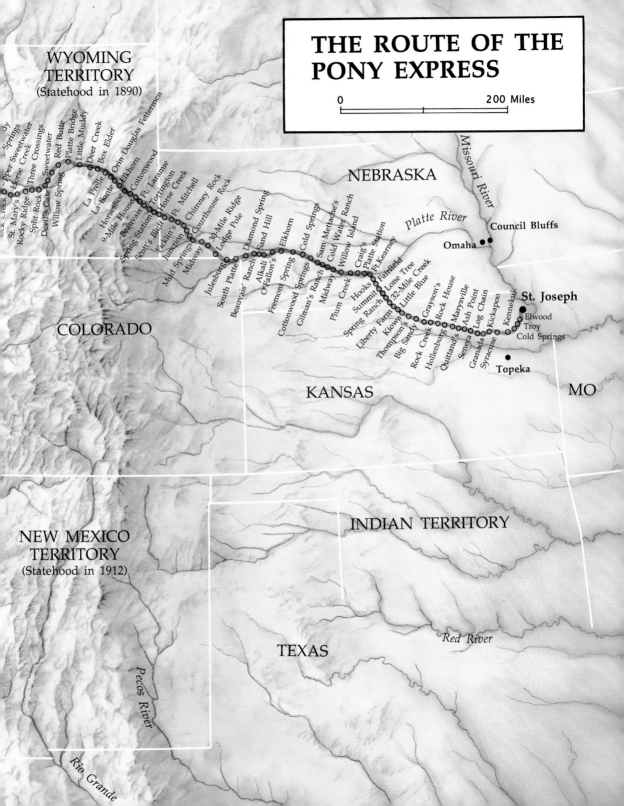

THE ROUTE OF THE PONY EXPRESS

0   200 Miles

WYOMING TERRITORY
(Statehood in 1890)

NEBRASKA

Platte River

Council Bluffs

Omaha

St. Joseph

Elwood
Troy
Cold Springs

COLORADO

KANSAS

Topeka

MO

Missouri River

NEW MEXICO TERRITORY
(Statehood in 1912)

INDIAN TERRITORY

TEXAS

Red River

Pecos River

Rio Grande

Upper Sweetwater
St. Mary's
Rocky Ridge
Horse Creek
Split Rock
Three Crossings
Devil's Gate
Sweetwater
Willow Spring
Red Butte
Platte Bridge
Little Muddy
Deer Creek
Box Elder
La Prelle
Orin Douglas Fettermen
La Bonte
Horseshoe
Elkhorn
9-Mile House
Cottonwood
Beauvais
Ft. Laramie
Spring Station
Torrington
Scott's Bluff
Ft. Mitchell
Horse Creek
Ficklin's
Junction
Chimney Rock
Courthouse Rock
Mud Springs
Midway
30-Mile Ridge
Lodge Pole
Julesburg
South Platte
Beauvais' Ranch
Diamond Spring
Alkali
Sand Hill
O'Fallon's
Elkhorn
Fremont Spring
Cottonwood Springs
Cold Springs
Gilman's Ranch
Sam Metitache's
Midway
Cold Water Ranch
Plum Creek
Willow Island
Craig's
Ft. Kearney
Hooks
Platte Station
Spring Ranch
Summit
Fairfield
32-Mile Creek
Lone Tree
Liberty Farm
Kiowa
Little Blue
Thompson's
Grayson's
Big Sandy
Rock Creek
Rock House
Hollenburg
Marysville
Quittand's
Ash Point
Seneca
Log Chain
Granada
Kickapoo
Syracuse
Kennekuk

Above: Relay stations housed fresh horses for riders carrying the mail across the frontier.

Left: The mochila was a leather saddle bag that carried letters.

tion. One could never be certain whether approaching hoofbeats were a Pony Express rider, a bandit, or a hostile Indian.

The company also had to establish home stations along the route. Like regular relay stations, home stations had horse stalls and a corral and a fresh horse waiting to carry the mail further along the route. However, when the rider arrived, he would remove the *mochila* from his horse and throw it over the saddle of the fresh horse, and a new rider would leap into the saddle and be off.

When the system was all assembled, Russell, Majors, and Waddell had put together 190 relay and home stations stretching across eight states, purchased about 420 horses, and hired 400 station men and women and 80 riders. Charges for mail delivery were five dollars for each half-ounce letter. Later this was reduced to one dollar. At first the mail run would be made once each week in both directions. Then management increased the service to twice each week.

Everything was set to go. The country waited to see if such a system could actually work. All that needed to happen now was for the young riders to make the journey and prove that the central route was, in fact, the fastest way to deliver the mail.

4 THE CHALLENGE OF THE LAND

The astounding distance of the Pony Express's 1,840-mile (2,960-km) route was itself enough to challenge the endurance of the sturdiest team of riders. But distance was only part of the challenge. The land along the way often put the courageous riders to the severest tests. Covering eight states—Missouri, Kansas, Colorado, Wyoming, Nebraska, Utah, Nevada, and California—Pony Express riders encountered nearly every type of natural surrounding imaginable, from roaring rivers to bone-dry deserts, and they experienced an equally varied array of weather conditions.

On his trek west, the first barrier the Pony Express rider met was what many a farmer called "Old Misery"—the Missouri River. Fortunately,

*A courageous rider taking off on the
first ride of the Pony Express*

*The Missouri River was one of
the first major obstacles Pony
Express riders had to overcome.*

the Pony Express riders were able to ride a paddlewheel ferryboat across the river to Elwood,
Kansas, part of the great Central Plains, where the
long lonely ride really began.

In his travels, the Pony Express rider eventually
arrived at the banks of the Big Blue River and
entered a more barren and rugged land. Once past
Big Blue, the rider continued west until he entered

a shallow valley that directed his progress to the north and Nebraska.

Here, to the rider's relief, the land was extremely flat, in contrast to the rugged area around the Big Blue River, in northern Kansas, and the endless dunes that lay ahead in the great valley of the Platte River.

Leaving the South Platte after fording its rapid waters at Julesburg, the journey headed northwest again and back to Nebraska.

Perhaps the most familiar sight on the Pony Express trail is one that can also be seen from many miles away. It has the appearance of an inverted funnel against the far horizon. Its name is Chimney Rock, and it signaled that the riders would soon be leaving Nebraska territory and entering the wild and magnificent realm of the Wyoming Rockies.

At this point, the riders knew that they were 80 miles (129 km) from Fort Laramie. But there would be other natural formations to gauge their progress. Not too long after leaving Chimney Rock, there appeared on the horizon what seemed to be a giant wall, a steep cliff barring the way west. This was Scotts Bluff, a huge rock formation nearly 1 mile (1.6 km) wide and 760 feet (472 km) above the Platte River. This massive obstruction had a great gash cutting through its center, known in later years

*Above: Chimney Rock, a natural formation in the
Nebraska Territory, signaled to riders that they
would soon be entering the majestic Wyoming
Rockies. Facing page, top: The Rocky Mountains.
Bottom: Scotts Bluff and the Mitchell Pass (center).*

as Mitchell Pass. As one approaches, Mitchell Pass turns out to be a narrow natural road through the great wall.

Shortly after leaving Mitchell Pass, the Pony Express trail climbed into the higher elevation of a new territory—Wyoming, an area of nearly 100,000 square miles (259,000 sq km). Here the rider found himself frequently crossing icy-cold streams that rushed with violent currents down a slope. From the near sea-level plains in eastern Nebraska, the riders had climbed over 7,000 feet (2,135 m) as they passed Fort Laramie. Onward the trail continued, until Independence Rock came clearly into view. Measuring over 5,000 feet (1,525 m) around and 193 feet (59 m) high, this granite rock became the "Great Record of the Desert." Thousands of emigrants on their way west climbed its sloped walls to engrave their names and dates for future historians.

From here on, the riders were ascending the steep grade up the Rockies. Eventually, the trail arrived at the great South Pass, a saddlelike terrain over which passed thousands of covered wagons on their way to Oregon and California. The trail would then head southwest into Utah territory.

As treacherous as the Pony Express trail was through the Rockies, the worst part was yet to

Independence Rock, a huge granite formation in the Wyoming territory, became a place for emigrants to engrave their names in stone recording their presence in the desert.

come. For now the trail led across hundreds of miles of desert, much of it salt flats and alkali dust, where no living creature could survive very long; where the acid dust and incredible heat could make one feel as though he was suffocating. Eventually the trail headed northwest and entered the Nevada territory. Here the trail meandered along the Humboldt River, then crossed the great Sink of Carson where wind-driven dust storms could blot out the sun and tear at one's skin like sandpaper. Or, just as suddenly, a rider could encounter an unusual dense fog that sometimes appeared in winter, covering the landscape with a mantle of ice crystals. It was a place where no green could be seen, a landscape of a hundred shades of brown against a vivid blue sky, a challenge to the very idea of living things. At this point the trail was heading southwest toward Carson City and the extremely hazardous Sierra Nevada mountain range. This was the toughest part of the Pony Express trail.

The Sierra Nevada is the largest unbroken mountain structure in the Pacific states, running about 400 miles (644 km) north and south. At some points, it is nearly 80 miles (129 km) wide, with hundreds of mountain peaks standing above 12,000 feet (3,660 m).

The Sierra Nevada Mountain Range was an extremely hazardous part of the Pony Express trail.

It was through this world of nature's giants that the Pony Express trail had to pass. Steep grades, narrow canyons, howling winds, frightening blizzards, incredibly deep drifts—all were barriers to the progress of even the most dedicated rider. Finally the trail reached its high point, where it looked down at Lake Tahoe. From here the trail descended down the California side of the mountains and once again into the desert. At last the trail ran through California, the promised land of the pioneers, the land of the great gold rush. Here the rider headed west to Sacramento where the *mochila* was placed on a paddlewheel ship for a trip down the Sacramento River to San Francisco—trail's end.

5 THE JOURNEY AND THE ADVENTURE

On April 3, 1860, both an Indian war and a civil war were brewing, one local, the other national. Both were to influence the Pony Express. The Indian war was a new and serious stumbling block, challenging the success of the service. But on that historic day in St. Joseph, Missouri, as well as in San Francisco, all thoughts were of a celebration for the brave young men who would hopefully make such a daring dream come true.

Crowds gathered in town to see the great event. Red, white, and blue bunting decorated the buildings. Flags flew on rooftops, bands played spirited music, and everyone was in a festive mood. On hand were the mayor of St. Joseph, Jeff Thompson, William Russell, and Alexander Majors, along with other dignitaries.

*St. Joseph, Missouri, the starting
point of the Pony Express*

Five P.M. soon arrived; the time that the first
rider was to carry the mail, including special mail
from the East, on the first leg of a long jouney west.
But the train carrying the mail to St. Joseph had not
yet arrived. Everyone waited . . . 5:30, 6:00, 6:30
. . . still no train.

At about 7:00 P.M. the distant sound of a train
whistle alerted the cheering crowd that the historic

moment was approaching. At 7:15, a cannon boomed the signal, and a young rider (no one is quite sure who the first rider actually was), dressed in a red shirt, blue trousers, fancy boots, and a buckskin jacket leaped onto his horse. With wild cheers ringing in his ears, he raced down the street a short distance to the *Denver*, a paddlewheel steamboat, which was waiting to carry him across the Missouri River to Elwood on the opposite shore in Kansas. As the ferry touched the shore, the rider was off and running through the desolate night toward the first relay station at Troy, Kansas.

Once again we come across the problem of lack of information or conflicting information. As was stated earlier, there were about 190 stations along the Pony Express route. However, the records of many of these stations were lost, and little or no information exists today to describe them or even substantiate their existence. To make things even more complicated, some stations had several names. Therefore, today, when historians come across a name for a station, they cannot be sure whether it is another relay station or simply a second name for a known station.

About one hour after he had left the ferry, the rider stopped at Troy station where he quickly threw the *mochila* on a fresh horse, which had been saddled by the stationkeeper, leaped onto the saddle, and was off at top speed toward Cold Springs.

The next relay station, Kennekuk, was located among a dozen houses, a general store, and a blacksmith shop. This was also a stagecoach stop and, therefore, one of the more comfortable places to encounter.

There is more confusion about the next station. Some sources list Kickapoo, some Goteschall, while others list Granada or several of these stations. But after that comes Log Chain, which is listed by most sources. This small station was located among a grove of beautiful elm, hickory, and walnut trees.

About eight hours after he had left the ferry, the rider arrived at the first home station going west—Seneca, some 77 miles (124 km) from St. Joseph.

This home station, which would be considered comfortable even by today's standards, was large, with many windows and a big porch. At this point, a fresh horse and a new rider carrried the *mochila* along the next leg of the Pony Express route.

The new rider's first relay station was either Ashpoint (according to some sources) or Guittard's, a small station where the only thing required was a fresh horse. About 10 miles (16 km) down the trail the rider arrived at the Hollenberg (sometimes called Cottonwood) station, a large wooden farmhouse-type structure.

Now the riders headed into Nebraska. The first relay station in Nebraska was Rock Creek. On through the Platte Valley continued the rider, finally arriving at Liberty Farm—a home station and welcome sight for the tired rider who would turn over his *mochila* to a fresh Pony Express rider.

Soon riders were in the western portion of Nebraska, stopping by stations with such localized names as Willow Springs, Midway, Cottonwood, Freemont Springs, where the stationkeeper's wife was struggling to raise a flock of chickens, and O'Fallon's Bluff, where a sign reminded weary travelers that they were now 400 miles (644 km) west of St. Joseph, Missouri. This also meant that there was still 1,500 miles (2,414 km) of Pony Express trail ahead.

The riders, now traveling along the south fork of the Platte River, were headed toward Colorado and the station of Julesburg. From Julesburg, the rider headed northwest, back through the western end of Nebraska, making a quick change of horses at Lodge Pole Creek. He certainly would not want to spend much time here, for the station was not much more than a large hole dug in the side of a hill with a crude front constructed of wood. There were two bunk beds for the station attendants, boxes for chairs, a tin wash basin, a pail of water, and a single public towel.

Mud Springs, the next relay station, was not much better; it was a sod shack with no extra sleeping accommodations. Still continuing west, the riders passed well-known landmarks, such as Chimney Rock and Courthouse Rock, climbing the 400-mile (644-km) steady grade into the skyscraping mountains of Wyoming where, in the middle of utter wilderness, suddenly appeared Fort Laramie.

For tired travelers who had come a great distance, Fort Laramie was a welcome sight, a place to rest, get a good meal, and to trade or replenish supplies. Here, one could buy steel beaver traps from England, mirrors from Germany, colored beads from Italy, calico cloth from France, gunpowder from Delaware, and the famous Hawken plains rifles from St. Louis, as well as food and whiskey.

Day and night the riders raced, through mountain passes with 15-foot (4.6-m) drifts and along desert flats broiling at 110 degrees F (43°C) in summer. The first station in Utah was Needle Rock, located near Coyote Creek in the barren foothills of the Rockies. A quick stop at Weber station, then across the Weber River bridge toward Salt Lake (City) station. Salt Lake House, located on Main Street in Salt Lake City, was a welcome relief for the riders. It was a comfortable home station with good food and sleeping quarters. After this stop, the land became extremely barren and barely livable, with water being so scarce that some stations had to have it brought in by pack mules from miles away. Rush Valley station was in such a location—a desolate, bone dry, flat land with not a single tree as far as the eye could see. The station was extremely small and built of stone.

From here on, the Pony Express riders entered the worst part of the trail and the worst desert in North America, also referred to as "Paiute Hell." The country was bare, with rocky mountain ranges, countless miles of parched sand, no vegetation, blinding dust storms, and bewildering mirages in the boiling summer, where even wild animals, other than snakes, seemed to refuse to live. There were large areas where the choking alkali covering the ground was so thick that it looked like snow.

It was with a tremendous sense of relief that a Pony Express rider reached the home station, Deep Creek. Here was a large, comfortable brick dwelling where a good meal, fresh water, and a soft bed awaited him. Next it was onto Nevada (at that time still known as the Utah territory). After that, the trail crossed the milder lands in California where the very comfortable station Sportsman Hall, with its clean rooms and delicious meals, delighted the weary rider. Finally the riders raced along the western end of the Pony Express trail. After nearly 2,000 unbelievable miles (2,725 km) and a historic journey, a young rider galloped into Sacramento, California, carrying mail from the eastern end of the United States. It was done in a record time of nine days and twenty-three hours.

The welcome at Sacramento was unforgettable. At 5:45 P.M. on April 13, 1860, the rider entered a town wild with joy and excitement. A holiday had been declared; buildings were decorated, people were on balconies and rooftops waving flags, there was singing and shouting, bells were jingled, and bands played as the rider (named Hamilton) was escorted to the Alta telegraph office where the mail was to be delivered. He had carried about eighty letters, including a letter of congratulations from President Buchanan to Governor Downey of California.

But the trip was not quite finished. There was still the San Francisco mail to be delivered. The large side-wheeler steamboat *Antelope* was waiting at the dock to carry the rider downriver. For a little while, the weary rider got some well-deserved rest. But then, as the boat approached the great California city, all the steamboats in San Francisco Bay began to sound their whistles in a wild welcome. It was close to midnight when the *Antelope* docked,

Top: Celebration welcoming Pony Express rider. Bottom: A Pony Express rider would meet the Antelope *at Sacramento and then proceed onto San Francisco.*

but the town was wide awake. It seemed as though all of San Francisco was there to greet the rider. Cannons were fired, rockets streaked through the sky, crowds cheered, and a vast procession formed at the ferry slip to escort the conquering hero into town. Bonfires were lit and crowds, holding torches, lined the streets. Even Jessie Benton, wife of the famous Pathfinder John C. Frémont, was there to welcome the Pony Express rider.

There was a wonderful sense of joy in the air. No longer was San Francisco an isolated town. Now the great city was a mere ten days away from the East by mail.

6

HEROES ON HORSES

"Wanted—young, skinny, wiry fellows not over eighteen. Must be expert riders, willing to risk death daily. Orphans preferred. Wages $25 per week." So read the posters that were put up around St. Joseph, Missouri, Sacramento, California, and other towns across the country. The Pony Express service was looking for very special young men, men who were willing to make great sacrifices, spending long hard hours in the saddle, riding through the black of night, in cold, in heat, and through life-threatening territories. They had to be totally dedicated to making certain that the mail would go through under any and all conditions.

Soon after the start of the Pony Express service, the fame of these brave young riders spread

WANTED

YOUNG SKINNY WIRY FELLOWS not over eighteen. Must be expert riders willing to risk death daily. Orphans preferred. WAGES $25 per week. Apply, *Central Overland Express, Alta Bldg., Montgomery St.*

Advertisements that appeared in San Francisco newspapers in March 1860

throughout the country. They were considered a very special class of citizens. Although they were young and small of stature, theirs was a big job— getting the *mochila*, filled with mail, across nearly two thousand miles (3,218 km) of wilderness.

The *mochila* was put on the saddle and held in place by the rider sitting on it. The *mochila* had four pockets called cantinas, one in each corner, so that two pockets were in the front of the rider's legs and two in the back. The cantinas were locked. Three of them could be opened only at the military forts and one by the stationkeepers. One of the pockets held a time card on which the stationkeepers would record the time that a rider arrived to change horses. A lot was expected of the riders, both in terms of their duty and their personal lives. In fact, every employee of the Central Overland California and Pike's Peak Express Company was required to take (and keep) the following pledge:

I [name], do hereby swear, before the Great and Living God, that during my engagement, and while I am an employee of Russell, Majors and Waddell, I will, under no circumstances, use profane language; that I will drink no intoxicating liquors; that I will not quarrel or fight with any other employee of the firm, and that in every respect I will conduct myself honestly, be faithful to my duties, and so direct all my acts as to win the confidence of my employer. So help me God.

This is not to say that all Pony Express riders were saintly men. But they were certainly devoted to their task and proved their loyalty over and over again. In their day, they were the heroes of our young nation.

Mark Twain, who in 1860 was making a trip across the country, mostly by stagecoach, captured the thrill and excitement connected with these young riders in his writings (titled *Roughing It*):

We had a consuming desire from the beginning, to see a pony rider; but somehow or other all that passed us, and all that met us managed to streak by in the night and so we heard only a whiz and a hail, and the swift phantom of the desert was gone before we could get our heads out of the windows. But now we were expecting one along any moment, and would see him in broad daylight. Presently the driver exclaims:
    "Here he comes!"

In Roughing It, *Mark Twain captured the thrill and excitement experienced by Pony Express riders.*

Every neck is stretched further and every eye strained wider away across the endless dead level of the prairie, a black speck appears against the sky, and it is plain that it moves. Well I should think so! In a second it becomes a horse and rider, rising and falling, rising and falling— sweeping toward us nearer and nearer growing more and more distinct, more and more sharply defined—nearer and still nearer, and the flutter of hoofs comes faintly to the ear—another instant a whoop and a hurrah from our upper deck, a wave of the rider's hands but no reply and man and horse burst past our excited faces and winging away like the belated fragment of a storm!

So sudden is it all, and so like a flash of unreal fancy, that but for a flake of white foam left quivering and perishing on a mail sack after the vision had flashed by and disappeared, we might have doubted whether we had seen any actual horse and man at all, maybe.

Perhaps the single word that best describes the Pony Express riders is "dedication." William Campbell, the last survivor of the Pony Express Riders, was faced with a threat to his life, wolves! One night, when he was riding along his route between Fort Kearny and Fort McPherson on Plum Creek, he came upon a big pack of large wolves feeding on a horse that they had just killed. When the rider dashed by, a number of the huge beasts took off after him, fully intending to bring down the horse because of their ravenous hunger. Unfortunately, Campbell had not brought his gun on that run and the next station was several miles away. The savage wolves were closing in on him. Things looked grave. There would be no way to fight off such vicious animals if the horse should be brought down. Suddenly, Campbell remembered the horn that he normally used to alert the stationkeeper of his arrival. Campbell took the horn and blew a mighty blast at the wolves. Startled, the pack stopped a moment, then continued their chase. As they approached, Campbell gave them another blast of the horn and once again they fell back. He was able to keep this up until he made it safely to the station.

At the stations, it was often equally or even more dangerous. One incident that took place at the height of the Paiute Indian War at the Egan Canyon Pony Express Station is a good example. One morning one of the stationkeepers named Albert Armstrong glanced out the window and cried out to his partner, Henry Woodville Wilson, "My God, Wood, it's Indians!" Even to the rugged frontiersmen the sight caused terror. Just outside the cabin was a full band of Ute Indians, all painted up and dressed for war. Armstrong and Wilson grabbed their rifles, fell to the floor, and fired away through several cracks in the old cabin wall. All too soon, their guns were empty and the Indians knew that they could safely approach the cabin. So they charged through the door, letting out terrible war cries.

By late afternoon, Armstrong and Wilson were tightly tied to stakes driven into the ground while the Ute warriors piled dried sagebrush around them.

The two men were paralyzed with fear, knowing that in a few minutes, flames would be burning them to a crisp. Then, to their amazement, there came the sound of charging horses. Next came the cracking sound of rifles firing and the panicked cries of the braves. The army troops, headed by Colonel E. J. Steptoe, had spotted the war party at the station and wasted no time in coming to the rescue.

It was this kind of danger that was ever-present in the minds of riders who rode the wild expanses of the Pony Express trail. Yet, these young courageous men were always ready to meet the challenge. And near the top of the list of heroes is the name Robert Haslam, known in history as Pony Bob, the rider who holds the record of the longest

*Alexander Majors is one of the men
who helped start the Pony Express.*

and fastest run in the history of the Pony Express. He had started out on his normal run, which was between Friday's station at the foot of Lake Tahoe, to Bucklands (later called Fort Churchill and also marked as Nevada on some maps). This was just about the time that the Pyramid Lake massacre was taking place and Indian war parties were roaming the entire area. Pony Bob reached Reed's station only to find that there were no fresh horses. They had all been taken by the local people to stage a campaign against the attacking Ute Indians. So Bob fed his horse and urged the tired beast on another 15 miles (24 km) to Bucklands station, where his 75-mile (121-km) run would be completed and he and the horse would have a well-earned rest.

However, when he arrived, Bob learned that the relief rider, Johnson Richardson, panic-stricken from the news that hostile Indians were on the warpath, refused to continue the run. This is the only recorded case of a Pony Express rider refusing to carry on the mail. As it happened, stationkeeper, W. C. Marley, was at the station. After giving up trying to convince Richardson to perform his duty, he turned to Pony Bob and offered him a fifty-dollar bonus to take the next run. Bob agreed, and ten minutes later, after checking his Spencer rifle and Colt revolver, he was off at a gallop. Ahead of him lay 35 lonesome, dangerous miles (56 km) to the Sink of Carson (shown on the map as Old River) station. Mile after tiring mile he rode, most of the time without a drop of water to drink. At Sink of Carson he changed horses and was off again on a 37-mile (60-km) trek over choking alkali wastes and parched sand until he reached Cold Springs station. Once again he changed horses and dashed off for another 30 miles (48 km) to Smith's Creek station (possibly marked as Castle Rock on some maps). With every muscle in his body aching, Pony Bob delivered his *mochila* to a relief rider, J. G. Kelly. Bob had ridden an unbelievable 190 miles (306 km) without stopping except to change horses. But that was not the end of his amazing story.

After several hours of rest, the west-bound rider arrived with the mail. So Pony Bob leaped on a fresh horse and raced back with the mail. After galloping 30 miles (48 km) he arrived at Cold Springs and a scene of tragedy. The stationkeeper had been killed by Indians and all the horses had been taken. The place was in ruins. Bob stayed only long enough for his horse to drink. Then he was away at top speed.

Eventually he arrived at Sand Springs station (marked Mountain Well on the map). He reported the raid on Cold Springs and convinced the stationkeeper that it would be far too dangerous to remain alone. So the two riders galloped west to the Sink of Carson (Old River) station. As it turned out, Bob had saved the man's life, since the station was attacked and destroyed the next morning. Waiting at the station were a group of frightened men who had just been attacked a couple of hours earlier by a Ute war party. With barely an hour's rest, Bob headed west on the Pony Express trail and arrived back at Bucklands (Nevada), only three and a half hours behind schedule. Pony Bob had ridden an incredible 380 miles (611 km).

The most famous of all the Pony Express riders was William F. Cody, better known as Buffalo Bill. Buffalo Bill was known throughout the world for his exciting Wild West show, with its real Indians, cowboys, buffalo, make-believe gunfights, trick riders, and Indians attacking wagon trains. Starring in the show was the famous western hero and subject of many western novels, Buffalo Bill. But success had not come easily to Cody: he had worked very hard for the things he had gotten.

Cody was born on February 26, 1845, in Scott County, Iowa. His father was a stagecoach driver. When young Bill was seven, the family moved to Missouri and two years later to Kansas where his

William F. Cody, also known as Buffalo Bill, was the most famous of the Pony Express riders.

father opened a small trading post. Then tragedy entered the young boy's life. His father, who believed that Kansas should be a free state (where slavery would not be allowed), was attacked and fatally stabbed by several Southern sympathizers.

At eleven years of age, Bill had to take over the duty of providing for his mother and younger brother.

Bill was barely fifteen when he managed, through a family friend, to get hired as a substitute Pony Express rider. After several months, during which time the lad maintained a good record, the regular rider returned and the boy had to move on.

With a letter of recommendation, Bill Cody approached none other than gun-totin' Jack Slade at Horseshoe Station. At first, the big gunfighter would not consider hiring such a skinny little kid. Then he read the letter and decided to give Bill a try. And as if he wanted the young lad to be discouraged, Slade assigned Bill Cody the 116-mile (187-km) route between Red Buttes and Three Crossings in Wyoming. It was a dangerous trail, with hostile Indians and bandits along the way.

On one trip, as Bill Cody arrived at Three Crossings, he learned that the rider who was supposed to carry the *mochila* westward had been killed the night before. Although Cody was very tired from his long run, he agreed to carry the mail to Rocky Ridge (St. Mary's), 76 miles (122 km) away. When he arrived at Rocky Ridge, he picked up the east-bound *mochila* and headed back to Red Buttes. He had ridden an amazing 384 miles (618 km) without a regular sleeping break. No one ever matched that record.

These are but a few of the many stories of courage and dedication that so well characterized the young Pony Express riders and the men and women who ran the relay stations.

PASSING INTO HISTORY

From the very moment of its birth on April 23, 1860, the days of the Pony Express were numbered, for other great events were about to appear on the stage of American frontier history. Nearly three decades earlier, a professor of art at New York University had invented an electric signaling system which, for several years, was considered little more than a laboratory curiosity by the United States government. He had to wait about ten years before the government gave him a chance to prove the benefits of such a system. In 1843, Samuel Morse was given the money to build a telegraph line between Washington, D.C., and Baltimore, Maryland. At its completion, the famous words "What hath God wrought" flashed across the wire and electrical communications became acceptable.

The construction of a national telegraph line in the early 1860s was only one of many events that shortened the life of the Pony Express. Just before the start of the service, the company that established the Pony Express had lost a great deal of money when a huge herd of freight oxen, used to pull large supply wagons, froze to death in a raging blizzard at Ruby Valley, Nevada.

Samuel Morse built a telegraph line between Washington, D.C., and Baltimore in 1843, heralding the age of wire and electrical communication.

The Indian war in the spring and summer of 1860 was another serious blow to the company. When the fires of war flared, many of the stations were burned to the ground, stationkeepers were killed, and equipment and horses were stolen. The cost to rebuild all this was $75,000, money that the company could ill afford to lose.

The Pony Express suffered because of the Indian War. Battles destroyed relay stations and took human lives.

Then came the awful winter of 1860–61 with its deep snows and unbearable storms. Many horses were injured because of the terribly hard riding conditions; they had to be replaced at a high cost.

By August 1861, most of the transcontinental telegraph line was completed. The western end of the line was already at Julesburg. A month later, only a few hundred miles separated the western and eastern crews building the line. The end of the Pony Express service was near. Then, on October 26, 1861, the wires on the line were connected.

The first message of congratulations was sent from Stephen J. Field, Chief Justice of California, to President Abraham Lincoln:

To Abraham Lincoln, President of the United States: In the temporary absence of the Governor of the State, I am requested to send you the first message which will be transmitted over the wires of the telegraph line which connects the Pacific with the Atlantic States. The people of California desire to congratulate you upon the completion of the great work. They believe that it will be the means of strengthening the attachment which binds both the East and the West to the Union, and they desire in this—the first message across the continent—to express their loyalty to the Union and their determination to stand by its Government on this its day of trial. They regard that Government with affection and will adhere to it under all fortunes—Stephen J. Field, Chief Justice of California.

During its eighteen months of service, the Pony Express had provided a dedicated and valuable service to the people of the United States. It had made a total of 308 complete runs, covering a distance of about 616,000 miles (995,000 km). That is equivalent to riding around the earth over thirty times. The riders delivered 34,753 letters over mountains and deserts, through snow and rain storms, during the day and at night, across raging rivers, and past fierce tribes of warring Indians. Only one *mochila* was lost.

The sentiments felt by the people for the unselfish service of the men and women of the Pony Express was best expressed in a newspaper article in the *Sacramento Daily Bee* on October 26, 1861:

FAREWELL PONY: *Our little friend, the Pony, is to run no more. "Stop it" is the order that has been issued by those in authority. Farewell and forever, thou staunch, wilderness-over-coming, swift-footed messenger. For the good thou hast done we praise thee; and, having run thy race, and accomplished all that was hoped for and*

NOTICE.

BY ORDERS FROM THE EAST,

THE PONY EXPRESS

WILL be DISCONTINUED.

The Last Pony coming this way left Atchinson, **Kansas**, yesterday.

(x25-1t **WELLS, FARGO & CO., Agents.**

expected, we can part with thy services without regret, because, and only because, in the progress of the age, in the advance of science and by the enterprise of capital, thou hast been superseded by a more subtle, active, but no more faithful, public servant. Thou wert the pioneer of a continent in the rapid transmission of intelligence between its peoples, and have dragged in your train the lightning itself, which, in good time, will be followed by steam communication by rail. Rest upon your honors; be satisfied with them, your destiny has been fulfilled—a new and higher power has superseded you. Nothing that has blood and sinews was able to overcome your energy and ardor; but a senseless, soulless thing that eats not, sleeps not, tires not—a thing that cannot distinguish space—that knows not the difference between a rod of ground and the circumference of the globe itself, has encompassed, overthrown and routed you. This is no disgrace, for flesh and blood cannot always war against the elements. Rest, then in peace; for thou hast run thy race, thou hast followed thy course, thou hast done the work that was given thee to do.

FOR FURTHER READING

Aylesworth, Thomas G. & Aylesworth, Virginia L. *The West*. New York: Chelsea House, 1988.

Collins, James L. *Exploring the American West*. New York: Franklin Watts, 1989.

McCall, Edith. *Mail Riders*. Chicago: Childrens Press, 1980.

Settle, Raymond W. & Settle, Mary L. *Saddles & Spurs: The Pony Express Saga*. Lincoln, Nebraska: University of Nebraska Press, 1972.

Stein, Conrad R. *The Story of the Pony Express*. Chicago: Childrens Press, 1981.

INDEX

Page numbers in *italics* refer to illustrations.

Antelope, steamboat, 38, 39
Armstrong, Albert, 46
Ashpoint station, 34

Baltimore, Maryland, 54
Benton, Jessie, 40
Bog Blue River, 22
Bravery of Pony Express riders, 49–53
Buchanan, James, 38
Bucklands station, 49, 51
Buffalo Bill. *See* Cody, William

Campbell, William, 45
Carson City, Nevada, 28
Central Overland California and Pike's Peak Express Company, 43

Chimney Rock, 23, *24*, 36
Cody, William *48*, 51, *52*, 53
Cold Springs station, 34, 50
Colton, John, *48*
Cottonwood station, 34, 35
Courthouse Rock, 36
Coyote Creek, 36

Dangers of Pony Express service, 45–53
Deep Creek station, 37
Delivery rates, Pony Express, 19
Denver, steamboat, 33
Downey, Governor, 38

Egan Canyon station, 46
Elwood, Kansas, 22, 33
End of Pony Express service, 54–60
Establishment of Pony Express service, 11–19

Field, Stephen J., 57–58
Fort Kearny, 45
Fort Laramie, 23, 26, 36
Fort Leavenworth, 13
Fort McPherson, 45
Freemont, John C., 40
Freemont Springs station, 35
Frequency of service, 19
Friday's station, 49

Goteschall station, 34
Granada station, 34
Guittard's station, 34
Gwin, William M., 13

Haslam, Robert, 47, *48*, 49–51
Hollenberg station, 34
Home stations, Pony Express, 19
Horseshoe station, 53
Humboldt River, 28

Inaugural trip, Pony Express, *21*, 31–40
Independence Rock, 26, *27*
Indian wars, 31, 46–51, 56
Ingraham, Prentiss, *48*

Julesburg, Colorado, 23, 35

Kelly, J. G., 50
Kennekuk station, 34
Kickapoo station, 34

Lake Tahoe, 30, 49
Length of Pony Express route, 14, 20
Liberty Valley station, 35

Lincoln, Abraham, 57
Lodge Pole Creek, 35
Log Chain station, 34

Mail service, demand for, 9–11
Majors, Alexander, 13, 14, 19, 31
Marley, W. C., 49
Midway station, 35
Missouri River, 20, *21*, 22, 33
Mitchell Pass, *25*, 26
Mochila (saddle bag), 15, *18*, 19, 30, 42–43
Morse, Samuel, 54, *55*
Mud Springs station, 35

Needle Rock, 36
New Orleans, Louisiana, *8*

O'Fallon's Bluff station, 35
Oregon Trail, 14

Paiute Indian War, 46
Platte River, 23, 35
Platte Valley, Nebraska, 35
Pledge signed by riders, 43
Plum Creek, 45
Pony Bob. *See* Haslam, Robert
Pony Express:
    dangers of, 45–53
    demand for, 9–11
    end of, 54–60
    establishment of, 11–19
    inaugural trip, *21*, 31–40
    riders, 15, 41–53
    route, 14, *16–17*, 20–30
    stations, 15, 33–37
Pyramid Lake massacre, 49

Rates, Pony Express, 19
Recruitment of Pony Express riders, 41, *42*
Red Buttes station, 53
Relay stations, 15, 19
Richardson, Johnson, 49
Riders, Pony Express, 15, 41–43
Rock Creek station, 35
Rocky Mountains, *25*, 26
Rocky Ridge station, 53
Roughing It, Mark Twain, *44*, 45
Route of Pony Express, 14, *16–17*, 20–30
Rush Valley station, 37
Russell, Majors and Waddell, 11–13
Russell, William, 11–13, 14, 19, 31

Sacramento, California, 30, 38, 41
Sacramento Daily Bee, 58–60
Sacramento River, 30
Saddle bag. *See Mochila*
St. Joseph, Missouri, 11, 14, 31, *32*, *34*, 38
Salt Lake House, 36
Salt Lake station, 36
Sand Springs station, 50
San Francisco, California, 14, 30, 31, 38–40
Scotts Bluff, 23–24, *25*, 26

Seneca station, 34
Sierra Nevada Mountains, 28, *29*
Sink of Carson station, 28, 50, 51
Slade, Jack, 53
Smith's Creek station, 50
South Pass, 26
Sportsman Hall station, 37
Stagecoach lines, 11
Station keepers, Pony Express, 15–19
Stations, Pony Express, 15, *18*, 33–37
Steam-engine trains, 11
Steptoe, E. J., 47

Telegraph lines, 11, 54
    transcontinental, 55–58
Thompson, Jeff, 31
Three Crossings station, 53
Troy, Kansas, 33
Troy station, 33
Twain, Mark, 43–45

Ute Indians, 46–47, 49, 51

Waddell, William, 13, 14
Washington, DC, 54
Willow Springs station, 35
Wilson, Henry Woodville, 46–47
Wolves, attack by, 45